The Blue Hour

POEMS

C . M . CLARK

Three Stars Press

ISBN 978-0-6151-6900-2

Acknowledgments:

Selected poems have appeared in the online journal *Asili*.

"Opening Day" appeared in *Gulf Stream* magazine, Volume 26.

Poems in "Between Sleep & Waking" appear in *Pillow Talk*, a collaboration with painter Georges LeBar.

Cover and Book Design by Pasita Andino.

In my life, I've loved you more...

for LA, AL & LO

Contents

Between Hell & High Water

Between Sleep & Waking

The Blue Hour

In Paris, they call it *l'heure bleu*, the blue
hour. Here we know it as dusk, an intermission
dyed umber and resin, faintly fragrant
from Old English, *dox*, dirt-brown, as in brown
earth and its dust. Is this because

across the rush of ships and mindless water, like time
between, we are all about the ground still?
What feigns above it
and festers below it
and by cellular affinity

belongs to it? Sea change?

Strange soil. It is in the corn
we pull from silk and chew, the pollen
that tinges the twilight, the air seeded
with brown ground, mulched
and fecund, that is not blue, but brusque --

not rarefied, not blue. Every blue hour

stands a century, gone centuries that glaze-buffed
the old burrs, the air
sandpapered and free from inclusions.
With day done, and evenings not yet ratified, sky
reigns clear, holding the snarling welterweights

of light and dark at bay. Step lightly.

It is treacherous

to walk on air.

Between the Devil
and the
Deep Blue Sea

Lineage

What ant walk along the concrete casement
and where headed while the air warmed and fattened
with scent.

The dogged parade to the heart of sweet, the lilt
and call of crumbs and honey -- leftovers
from my jelly bread – inland

caravans determined and indefatigable, the sash
ledge, the wide flat world beyond the knitted screen,
where globed carved cheek rests

still to be intuited. Plateau of mica schist
and sludged concrete, knowing

only the call, a lure of crumbled candy.

I could follow that line forever, at least
until the rain stops. But the trekking
singlenoted step-like stitches

hem-basted brings the boiling water

stew pot, flushing their channel

crossing, like pepper pouring over winterbrick. Could

no crevices hide the last one, inverted
prometheus knot? The deep dreams, to hide
in the thunderheads, the wounds

of rain

unforecasted, languidly sanctioned. A simple
coexistence of my matter
and theirs

exoskeletal reminder of fragile snail lugging
shy cell on serious back. Serious
but feeling the weight, and urging

the sand to part

like so much red sea.

Last Dibs

Ante up. The cards land before my face, face drawn
down and puckered with the rising smoke, the pensive sigh, wishing
for that better hand all night. The night

is no longer young, young

and moist as you, old like me, and already
so disappointed. This afternoon was perfect in its remembering
reminding us why we submit to wild edges, agricultural plots

strawberries in fullness sweet bites saturating

a large, tonsiled mouthful, though I try to hide
my teeth, uneven and creased with pulp, yet
the wet chin's worth it, worthwhile and so succulent, so

smileworthy.

Fair

Swing low, sweet circumstances of late year Saturday, late
rising morning, early pearl grey shifting
substance cobwebs and voile curtains. Anxieties

fleet on the tailfeathers

larval with mosquitoes that stir and hum, hatch
awake uncertainly, then footsteps on hardwood
in sunlight

a light voice on the phone.

Alone in sleep's tidepools unswayed by moon
or magic, the promised headache that strums
cloudstrings like eagles' talons

dissipates. Slurring rhythms of cats' teeth chewing,

a low-tuned radio, lighter than catastrophe
instead plays favorites, afterschool specials
and the forecast, after midday showers

a general clearing, with chances of rain

greatly diminished.

The Death of Jane Kenyon

She makes a handsome run of it, a gloved handful's
grab with one hand clapping, some summer's firefly
half-life incandescence jar-trapped, subtle

seedless grapes served as dessert – pale and white green

from California. Sweet bites before evening

falls.

I know if I just held her head, maybe touched
the fine bones beneath the scalp's robin-feathering, or
smoothed the last swirls of rabbit grey, last

light in the autumn sky or
stood champion beside the basin as she upswilled
poison, expelled cells that sank

life's buoyancy, leadened down
her words, compromised her walk, matted
her cancer

hair.

Entering the honeycomb of language, delectable byways but
I can't find you among these prisonyard turns,
ruins, sanctioned release beyond the barbed wire, Jane. Remaining

a tear of paisley hem, tortoiseshell
toggle button, graphite shavings and random false starts under
erasure. They will study you

under imagery. Find you in an extra copy left
on the desk after class's

dismissal.

Where does this leave me? I plucked
words in season from bramble bushes, the brackish
silk weeds, sea oats by bay's salt side

suckled on orange blossoms and rind, even
the bitter sap stirred my taste, one day
in hiding, taken out of context, light from

light.

Hildegard & the Rising Fifth

[Hildegard of Bingen was a 12th Century writer and composer of
unforgettable choral music which brought church plainchant to a highly
individual art. Her use of the ascending fifth, rather uncommon in earlier
liturgical pieces, became her signature, her thumbprint.]

It's a turn of phrase
just a lilt of notes that soars
through this old stone, the choir's eagle's nest,
the spectrum shift of leaded glass that moves you. Memories

hatch like ducklings. It wasn't always this way. Memories

of morning hours outside Mainz, warm
with milk and shadowing belled cows,
ox-eyed daisies – symphonies of the painted season.

Disembodied leaves of birch and elm in autumn, the scoop and fly
when heat returns to hills' climb. Sweat, your muddied hems,
and the smell of slow beasts and umber soil rich in iron. The iron

convent gates wax-sealed the silence, the stiffening, a stifling death

in life until the voices,

their gathered voices break
fast like flutes or
soft-strung lyres
rising as wood smoke through braided thatch,
song-shaped,
the iconic air of assembled days.

It's a croon of hum
just an arch of breath that ascends with the sparrows, invisible
spirit-space, without predefined length or width, where pointed spires
press heaven. You remember

the wind in winter, whistling, with cold feet,
the inside drafts, the drifts
like fallen clouds. They say

it was visions, a dream of singing angels in tiaras
with sparkling rings, one for each finger
echoing the shine of virgins, their hair unbound.

But no. You remember

human women with baskets of dried fruit, chewing cherry bark, men
with hatchets, hewing pine, massaging pitch and tar,
their baritones chest-deep in desiduous leaves,

and always the singing hands at work, mostly your mother's
smoothing stubborn hair, the voices weaving ribbons and yarn-spun
bows,
the surprise when the shyest girl hits

the highest note

with dazzling splendor.

With Kid Gloves

Late year invites spring cleaning. Tap rooting
through old calendars, cards
for birthdays I can't recall, condolences

for a loss vague-blurred. So embarrassing, death, so
signatures are softspoken, muted beige wildflowers,
rainbows in pastel diminuendo, and wide

angle views of a beach emptied of day's long

spoils. Visual pearl

that grows from one sand grain embedded
in mollusk flesh, layer
after layer of opalescence numbing the pang.

What color, what original land's end, what wave
or neap tide, lodged that irritant, undetectable
invisible to catscans and reminiscence. The pearl flirts

with my skin tones. A bracelet to catch the light, and move

gloved, with my hand's every gesture.

The C-100A

Across the canal, the culvert punctures
seeping bank and coral ridge, the rise
and fall of brackish water. Across my sightline

where sandbags bricklaid slap the side row of drain

pipe, safe-sided channel for muskogees
and coots' caw, the occasional turtle and air-despairing
fish that fly three times wide

decrying their underwater path

most promising. Across the interplay of species, my pool
surreal blue dreamqueen blue
and bluer than the mucktide

bottom aligning my property's short half

acre, each square inch's turf mortgaged,
mine. And all I can think of, sight
unseen across the sun sky's transit

is breathing blue, called

to be bluer by chlorine, infused and carbon
cleaned through to the particled bottom, though
I know any gill-dreamed last gasp of mine

will be shorter

sweeter like life among the brown roots,
the blooming algae.

Metallica

Truckload of flattened cars, just
remnants of onetime particularity
visible – individual
fingerprints of vehicular
living – like a loved pet, white
hood once simonized
adoringly, something sleekly chrome
crushed, something
that was two-
toned, or maybe a mismatched
door badly fashioned to fit the missing
passenger's side. What lives, karmic
juices stirred? First
dates? Last days
of school? The way there
to a new job, new
life in a new
city, tags changed to protect
the innocent? Where is
your car? Hand me
down of a hand me
down. And now you
too will change plates,
sending home the one
I'd rise for, live
for, seeing it in the driveway, or
there on the lawn occupying its
place in the sun when

I left for work
early, you home late
still asleep in the guest room.
You sent that plate back; what revisioned
ideogram of code, random alpha-numeric mix now
and from where? The land
of Lincoln now? No longer
the sunshine
state, no longer the sunshine at all?
Just flat old cars trucked to a heap. The best
we can hope for are memories of joy
riding, and the recycling
of metals.

Snails, Worms, and Other Losses

caught live food that squeals against my molars

must be French, it seemed, hearing the garlic cut
caper across the breath, the gristled globes swimming
tide's shallows one minute, cast

iron skillet chef's thumbpinch the next. Not

your inching creature, mazed in silica
curls, a curved fairweather pink castle
in the round, but slow roadkill

fast food to feed the yen for escargot
to go. Slick snack not found on my shelf, snail's loss
my lack, my gain. My teeth throat belly await

their diet al dente vermicelli, but better luck
had here with butter, or better yet olive oil's extra
virgin press. See, this I can

cook in my kitchen, nothing

harder than boiling water, spiked
fist of salt, and time. What was once
plainfield wheat now snakes the dance

of worms. How far have we come

really? Unless wrapped in cellophane, roused
cell memories of mastadon (hold the bun)
blanch: bone-breached and bald, but like hair like

life, losses are meant to be

cut.

Snow. Man.

Here, snow takes on the manswagger
of myth, straggling and chap-clad, the dirt
and dirge of slush

and slung-back heels glazed by snowplow
salt, grim-weathered and blunted gray. Here,
you dream in drifts, fakefur-skinned

and snowblind, deaf to omens that the iceman
cometh. Heatstroke
shapeshifts here, frostbite's striptease

imagining all that
white's just witnessed cloud gone
to ground with sizable

accumulation. Here, snow's

man's miracle, manufactured. Or one
rare morning, chilled and hovering
at freezepoint, apocryphal reminder

where you were when hell froze

over. But in July and such,

when you loll in calla lilies, and locusts
dervish-whirl through silk dusk, the snow
daze seems distant, and as much

fever-burn as freezer-bruise:

intangible leftovers, like twin anjou pears
dented black with insistent prodding, waiting
to defrost the spell, delete

the irreducible snowman.

Sick Days

In their juvenalia, he holds her, clear
and fearless of fever's catching, rattling clavicles,
damp forehead chill. Under sweltering blankets

hot darkness,

she patiently sweats. Slats

of blinds screen out blade's glare, beads
percolate in sheet creases, sour linens, yet
morning hours later, grimace gone, gone

like stealth, he leaves, elastic,
all joint aches tamed

in his pocket, hip-deep.

Sea-level

High in the oaks and the dogwood
Flattened hum of forest floor
Trading patches of last sun illumination
For shadowed day's done.
Dusk's brown sifts from stirred leaves pointing
The bear's path to bird-feeder secreting corn flecks,
Unseeded sunflower.
Bowers break along the eloping claw tread
The gamey trek through rising breeze
Shifts the air's scent, where tang of human meets
The wild fur, wet fang.
Foraging and farming crossing paths.
Mountain montage moues and mutates;
Unsettling vertigos of quick-change lift,
Lofty altitude. Huff and hunger for valley floor
Undoes the inner ear.
Out of my element, grazing the peaks --
Vistas too wide for scurrying astigmatism
Uncorrectable.

I shift my gaze to the hermit crab
Land-prone itinerant, borrowed baggage.
Craven and familial, we set our sights
At sea-level, where nothing wilder to sniff settles
Than an abandoned whelk,
A cracked conch
Waiting for the nearest wave
Or an outgoing tide.

In All That Rain
(after Robert Hass)

In all that rain
a truculent snail traveled my door frame
making its slow way in vain to drier wood
and safety. Between squall lines
I cracked the door, dislodging
prehistoric shell and the creature within now
gone clattering to ground,
calcified barracks barreling through dark pools.
The next morning, ants
were already at work
scavenging for days ahead. Rainy days.
I shoe-swept their leavings into the grass, just some
buried corpse in mother-of-pearl, a slow seed.
By night, the rain subsided,
a dead moth now near my chair,
folded in half, as in life, almost,
unmoving.
I don't know whether the cats toyed it to cabin-fever death,
or just fatigue harbored beating against the wind-waves,
in vain.
I left it – all geometric precision –
my reminder
for what might have been:
a small triumphant triangle of black and yellow
and stillness.

The Idylls of Bloomington

I stream down the last hill with the night highway, dreaming
Down through the side aisles of full-fed forest
Down into the valley of the Ohio.
The summer soils rich with vines and ox-eyed daisies,
And silk fingers of plumping corn.
Coursing ghosts of fog, swimming
Low across the horizon
Leaping the median
And into the headlights
In milky ribbons of smoke
And intangible floss.
A dance of dervishes, caught and scattered
With each skipping mile.

To be inland like the river
Is a fulsome contentment.
Far from the sea and the sea birds flying
Far from the salt air and the salt-shocked water
Far from the shoreline limning the country
Miles and mileposts from the mutable boundaries
Dividing dry land from wet ocean,
Impossible me from impassable you.

In this generous valley, no answer is needed,
The questions irrelevant.
Just fertile field following hill-wound road
And full various green ignoring gravity
Heedless of limits
Pushing summer-ward toward cloud-streaming sky.

This could be my last premeditated visit, dreaming
A final defined reason to fly from unsettling uncertainty.
To wake with the tender morning bound by the crossroads,
But fully free to choose the next destination
The next town's town limits,
Fully present and perfectly anonymous.

The next time I come, I will come to stay
Establish a life, choose an address,
Devise a new name to be known by,
And fed and bedded down safely
I will dream dreamless
Drink coffee at sunrise
Embroider fictions across a sunlit porch, unheeded,
The surprising quietude of Queen Anne's lace along the railing,
A roseate mandala among weeds, unseen.

Next time I travel, I will leave my bags behind, unneeded,
Traveling light into light
Following the hills and the land's contours
Streaming down through the trees, dreaming,
Steering focused and awake
All night, down into the valley of the wide rushing river.

Midwinter Spring

Sitting here in the coldfire sun
content with the choice
the choosing.

The park in late winter, cold
leaching surfaceward
from the ground up, groundling

the new grass. I fit -- arrow
in quick quiver --
my shape and turn in warmed burrows. Air

still so chilled still a little
nasty-bright, sharp
with the breeze. Today's much

the same. Though more latitude-friendly
this sun, this much sooner stop
for the spring-woken trip. Then

as now, no one visible, only voices
periphery-spread down the busway, the thick-throated el
up the canal. Boat's hum causes

pause. Smoothing the way, chevron wake wraps silk

for ducks, floating coconuts, sun's fingerprints.

Spring Coat

I.

It's so early for the bougainvillea, too soon
for so much magenta, so many
petals, such crepe twirling tissued streamers

in the gym. Just a day, like the last dance before
graduation, before
summer. The theme

was "Spring Fever," a virus
we'd all catch, like herpes
from a kiss, and chronic. The symptoms

only are treatable. My faceless future
susceptible, fingertips without
prints. It's ventricular

the gong of sudden
longing, and hidden
inside the pregnant

pause, two skips, skipped
beats of my tiring heart.

II.

Driving north. My mother's bones
call out across tomato fields, farm
earth bit in furrows fallow

for now, recovering
by doses of ancient
nitrogen. Waste

not, want
not.

III.

In the spring rain, so sudden
the creped green, blows wild like hair left
hanging, caught sodden

not nearly as tacit and hemmed,
as loomed or woven, invoking
this burgeoning chlorophyll. The birds sit sharp-

eyed to windward, poised to hear
the next sheet drenching sidewards,
clustered on branches, still sullen

tangled bare: an ancient heartbreak caught
in robe and rollers glaring, shuffling mules weighing
the competition, newborn and wet,

fresh. In the spring, they plant trees

still with tags tied, matching costumes laundered
and conscientious. As soon as the cloud
passes, comes the chorus of oily drops and wet wings

birdsong and wind-dried fenceposts,
treebark and empty corners,
vacated wires,

the whirr of feathers.

IV.

Spring coat on my lap, two sides of the split
season, satin
and wool.

I wore my spring coat too soon, the late
winter bitter, bitten, and too long
into warm weather. But I loved it,

winter white, spring clean, sharp
lapels and buttons,
the heft and hew of virgin lilac.

You are like spring: poignant and brief.
One day I wake up, and all colored
petals glue the ground. Pretty stamps

from foreign countries. Outside my front door
everything is green, green only. So much
life, photosynthesis ongoing, whether I care

or not.

Between a Rock
and a
Hard Place

Forgetting to Remember

"And I will show you fear in a handful of dust..."
T.S. Eliot, *The Waste Land*

When I buried my mother
It was a sweet September afternoon
Of crepe myrtle and hibiscus,
Midway between the mournful hours
Of brutal morning's indifferent sunrise
And the sloe-eyed moonless night,
Halfway between one blind storm's barbarous bark
And the next, fast and furious on its backsliding heels.
And she had no need to catch her breath as I did
From the ups and downs of corrugated paneling,
The needling tattoo of abused dead branches.
No need to catch her breath,
And no breath to catch,
Caught up in that devolution of flesh
And the sonic boom break-free
Of hightailing life loosened.

When I buried my mother
The caravan formed like the blind-man's bluff
Of eager traders,
But there were no pearls and spices
At this silk road's end.
Only a cool pool and indulgent shy trees
To convince the living
That death is a sweet afternoon in mid-September.

When I buried my mother
I remembered to follow the rules of generations.
A portico-covered plot in the graveyard's new ground,
Folding whitewashed chairs for the family,
Matinee front-row seats,
Where every mourner hand-cups
A handful of soil
To begin the hands-on labor of covering traces,
Trails and cornices of lathed wood,
Fine-grained pine.

When I buried my mother
I saw her set on her way.
A pioneer of atomic ash and molecular-bond
Broken elements
And my handful of dust,
A breadcrumb path to September's sore core,
The eyewall's counterclockwise circling space
Of momentary stasis,
Before the backlashing dirty side
Spawned cyclonic vacuums
To suck the residue of sweet recollection
Out of sight
And out of mind.

Hurricane Season

I.

I am pregnant with panic, and sick
with saline dysfunction,
looming departures, no safe cell.
The atmosphere is unstable, self-fulfilling center well
repository of endless discomfort,
ever replenishing, like breastmilk
coagulating on demand,
with an aftertaste, an inflection of salt.
Blind ellipsis of salt and dirty ocean,
endless loss, losing hours of autumn light,
spasms of birdcalls,
an invisible partner sleeping elsewhere
and the night sweats,
the sweat beading your face
the song
the heat that longs to break
as sweat.
I am deathly allergic,
encoded with saline pathology,
craving the soft, the sweet,
the molten honey.

II.

The bloom is off the rose; exhausted
the petals wane. Moons and mornings
follow fast, moisture beading on skinned tissue,
flowering fingers until juices escape
dissipated into the thinning thinned air.
Lazy heads droop on sallow stalks
thinning hair flying with the thin breeze
barely noticeable, noticed.
All nourishing water absorbed, evaporated
until there is no point.
Fear and fatigue in equal measure
fold the hand.

III.

The fragrance of her clothes enthralls me
nauseates me.
How long before the familiar perfume that clings to the cloth
vaporizes
and all that's left is fiber and faded fabric,
some cleaned chemically shrouded in plastic sheeting
others still trumpeting stains of a forgotten meal
tomato-based, dead-sea salt-seasoned,
ineradicable.

The last limp coat left hanging, forgotten
when the useless striped shirts and shorts
are removed, reassigned,
tucked in one pocket's recess, one wadded tissue
and a brush,
to settle the static stubborn hair
now caught threads, detached and rootless,
silk inelastic,
fully greyed, still bristle-wound,
inhaled irresistably to detect whatever was lost
lingering. Impossibly
gone but somehow still
the genome pool, simulation
of elusive helix
the dried residue of remembering
catches in my throat like spring pollen,
dust of dandelion and embryonic goldenrod,
dander released to air, faded,
first insatiable delirium, until
finally stasis,
the still dust of pressed flowers,
letting go.

IV.

I am the queen of the dead roses
caught between velvet petals remembered
and the drifting dust of afternoon bleached in haze.
Respiring aimless residue's drift of energy
and matter
material bonds of broken carbon
loosened
gone to ground.
Grounded, landlocked at last
(the sea stirs elsewhere),
I dream of closure
a last page
an end-stopped sentence
the clear humility
of sweet water.

Hard Times in the Big Easy & Elsewhere

In the jambalaya stew that is New Orleans, they bury their dead
Aboveground.
A last landing rest at fictional groundlevel
Eight feet below beyond sea reach
Held dry, held back with whisked walls
All carnivalesque and potpourri,
A simmering roue of rock aggregate formed formal
For a time
But only for a time as the crow flies.
Along St. Charles today, the dowagers hike their sodden shifts
Slanting kohl-caved eyes bruised and cloud closed
Inured to the swimming sarcophagus sea
Suddenly awash with Bourbon totems and viaticum –
Food fast for the last savory journey
The long Acadian decline, delta down.

Come with me down the delta,
Let's storm the soaked citadel,
The tangled footpath of loosed cats still meandering
And poking for loitering three-legged lizards
As yet unrelieved of their blatant red glottis.
Obscene protein.
Secret sweet meat.

They always eat and run
And always leave what has always been indigestible.
Now, my pet, she favored squirrel.
Also red-shouldered blackbirds so self-confessed
So deaf to stealth, so dead.
She strayed invisible in the wreckage, the frantic search and rescue
And re-emerged before dawn one Tuesday
One unobserved moment, stiffened in bas relief on the asphalt,
An Egyptian feline frieze
Frozen. Hieroglyphic triumphant defying
Decoding. Champollion!
Champollion! Uncork your wisdom and decipher my stone
My grief mouthed in three lost tongues
Before the trash truck rumbles down midmorning
Before my cat cartouche joins the club
Of plate-scraped rice and chili gumbo.
Empty cans and carcasses restored to the elements
Without benefit of clergy
Missing amazing grace,
The shadow purr and yowl lifting towards the eaves' hollow
The front porch unprowled
In too sudden twilight.

Evening hours sift unrecorded with Arcadia compromised.
Broken glass in vacant lots, no crops
Yield in debris fields,

However long left fallow
And frustratingly flat.
But these landfills compost my molehills
My mountains
My surrogate ground.
Pregnant bellies and plowed catacombs.
The silence of scavengers.
So the time came round
When my mother wound our songless songbird in silks
And carried those still sharp markings
Those flightless wings tucked in cardboard, a solitary cortege
Through the winter park. The recalcitrant soil
She dug, a box-shaped hole, a bird choir cabaret
To serenade shiftless survivors every second Sunday.
Then back home empty-handed, emptying the empty cage
Of stained newsprint,
Delinquent feathers.

Feathers stirred and stilled and settled,
Hovering ibises stalk their ground
Where ground remains.
Dance of twigs and eye-gleam –
Requiem of diaspora,
Lullaby of return.
Now my father wants me to help tend her grave, her home

Add sod, pull weeds, water
Where the drought bites,
All to preserve a bit of bitter ground
Designed to snakebite impermanence.
The old survivor's song refrain,
Purse our whistling lips in the storm's eye,
Brush worm's-mouth crumbs from granite tablets.
How far down beneath the topsoil
Does she own?
What lawn left to mow?
Dispossessed, disenfranchised
She is the reigning queen of plot seventeen –
Prudent. Compassionate. Kind to beggars
And ownerless strays.
Gloriana suburbia –
In with the flood,
Out like a light.

I want to leave loose as air
Leaving no relic to consecrate
No lock of hair, no shred of blouse to mourn,
No defined coordinates for weeping weekend visits.
Just space and sky –
And impossible blue flying the storm's morning after.
Just more dreaming west with sundown
Across the bayou's hum,
And purged of morbid grey and water gore,
Just a cloud, heliotropic, thinned with light.

The Last of the Cruzes

My mother was not the last of the Cruzes. That footnote
was held for her sister Rose, holding out gaggle-toothed until all
   ledger entries
nested with grandkids in half truths, piecemeal menus

of miscarriages, birthday cards in bloom, *a la carte*, year

after year.

After years

of private traumas, tumors, and bleak vituperatives laid public,
   they haunt
the boiler-room, the screened-in root kitchen, the basement
cinder block and cellar red brick, iron stained

and sullen with swollen hauteur.

They played kind, offering *hors d'ouevres* crumbling, and courtesy
and like all kin, swallowed leftovers

bland and

tone deaf.

The two sisters fought over the greater good of elderly parents,
the better half of a used upright piano. Their zealous
jealousy prompting my father -- Solomonic in rage

and Norsely Thor-like hiking his hammer –

to smash the ivories back to whale's teeth
and tusk, again. In death
the family convened for the last child

the lost chord struck, a full measure, misty
and elegiac music wide enough to gather the waltzes,

the random foxtrot,

solid with verve and sidestreet accents to linger
longer than Indian summer, diamond
nicked by the grooves, traveling

78 revolutions
per minute.

End of the World, End of the Road

Waiting
for the other shoe to fall
the night reclines, the call that doesn't come
gums the wires, the works.
Still she lives to breathe, pinwheel eyes to spin
to last to see another day.
Untucking sheetsail bedlinen, disavowed feet forgetting
the mud that clots the clogs, the dressy pumps,
the showy patents, the crosstrainers, prescribed,
paired, primped
for hypothetical strolls around the duck pond.
It is late August; even the sky sweats.

Waiting
for both shoes to land
just inside the front door threshold.
Until then stuck in sleep with one eye open, sleep
sticking in eye corners, gluing cells to soul, locking
slumberers in shots three-quarters over
the left shoulder, framing unlikely rendezvous
with fictional co-stars, living and dead.
All casts accounted for at last
as the tape rolls and the dreams unwind their surly dance,
unscripted games. Real life ringelevio at great risk
before your midnight snack and the sigh of your pillow.
And for me, it was all dusk and dinner: until,
home free all.

Waiting
for the other shoe to return
from the hereafter, from the dead zone
of storms past. From mired storage
a Cinderella pink slipper, a souvenir
for untried toes, left behind by the years' antic press
and the relentless blindwash, today
unpacked from flood debris dripping
sediment, the brackish breach of land by sea.
Insinuating through the pine roof timbers strapped down
and sidling the walls that hold the wind
the wet seeps, coloring
the mementos and the memories
in the hue of water.
One shoe uneasy, seeking its misplaced mate, mismatched
with other token totems I rescue:
a once-worn outgrown dress, some sundry game
with pieces missing,
lock of hair, lost tooth,
comely carbon relics to embroider the altar, receding
like some renegade hairline – the retreating
sighing surge spent.

Waiting
to hang up my intentions, my spurs,
and tiptoe unseen onto sacred ground, succumbing

to the bells of endless Sunday
and the sheer grass of daytime --
soft gravel's grace. I engage my middle age
in middle earth with both feet bare
ascending the hillside, human heels
in the promised land, while you fly
longlost kites that scan and map
beyond the unreadable harbor.
We are just a handful of barefoot contessas:
equally acquitted – equally forbearing of all calloused jeopardy,
All ungarnished sky.

The Doll Collector

My mother is a lanky, life-sized doll,
A skeleton beneath skin.
Clothed in rags, mismatched crumpled gown
Over gown, patchwork of prints
Assembled by colorblind penny-an-hour day laborers
In an Asian city with a name unpronounceable
By Western tongues.
Her doll-bright eyes blinded by the opening moment
Focus into mine, and recognition unfolds.
She has had her bath. She grew grey late
And now her clean-flying hair barely covers
Her doll-head scalp, scandalously virgin
And frighteningly young. Newborn
Transparency, intermittent as the flickering screen
Of nightly sitcoms, made-for-tv mysteries,
Sober hand-held documentaries filmed
When the world was black & white.
A grin of gums greets me; she remembers my name
Remembers the reciprocity of pushing my brass-polished carriage
Bundled in blankets for winter's bite,
As I push her wheeling throne
Through the shadier pavements of August.

In the dream, my baby doll melted to nightmare rubber,
A grave-stolen, decomposing face
Facing mine on the pillow.
But she stormed that terror
And the nightlight restored my incandescent world to daydream,
And my mute toy's pouting lips
To kissable plastic once more.

In the dream, she was the toy that slept
On a towering terrace, convalescing.
Squinting in the noon light, my father urged me from far below
To hurl her home,
Hoist her bulk over the rail
Where he waited to catch her.
Misgivings sparked like acid jolts;
But this was just a doll –
Large as life perhaps –
But not my warrior-protector
Horn-helmeted Valkyrie singing
Coloratura chants to vanquish slithering snakes
Beneath the surface of my clean wash-bright days.
So I pitched her overboard into the waves of charged air
Where she swam graceful as an air-breathing seal
In her element. But his strong arms

Missed. Neither wide enough, nor quick
To embrace this bundle of flawed defiance,
And on impact, she was my mother again.
My defender defenseless against gravity
And the avalanche of snow-weight
And inevitable ground.

When I was a child, my favorite doll
Long lived lost behind a high curtain rod,
While she was replaced with an inferior copy
For years, until we moved, dismantled the draperies,
And found her dusty
And hungry
And still bright-eyed,
Although my time for dolls had passed.

Some childhood playthings are irreplaceable. Pray
Though we do nightly,
Our best-loved toys lost in the years,
As nightmare's ferocity
Leaks through the dawn hours
Unending even when we must finally
Put all dolls away in dusty boxes
And awake.

Opening Day

My father is a natural lefty -- dyed-in-the-wool, fruit-of-the-loom --
though he writes and reads right. Called in those days a switch-hitter, a
two-fisted, pants-on-hips-slung hard-footed offensive menace, the kind
that could push and pull like a heartache, northwest by northeast, or
whichever way the pitcher's heat came spit-slick toward him.

Now spring heat is one tricky, dusty, untrustworthy thing, makes me want
to wanderlust away to the perfect afternoon of red clay and seismological
diamonds etched in acres of April come again.

Spring training seeds such dandelions and deliriums. Arouses glove-
leather to bead, as teenage Iliads and Odysseys secrete unknowingly
sanctifying the hubris of the first training bra, the Gotterdammerung
of first period algebra, the Greek chorus of boys who sweat and shave
and use cologne, evaporate and precipitate as particles ladling the fresh
field, the foul lines freshly sprayed defining the frontiers of balls played,
plowed fair.

On the one dusty day my father swung from the left, itching to oust
the winterkinks, unfurl the POW in pulverize, he pulled that first low
curve foul. Connect he did, bat on ball, ball sideswiping the carbonized
afternoon air, catching the still soft skullbones of some blond kid's left
temple. Left, then right to the ambulance blailing, called frantically.
Game called on account of darkness.

Most vivid though the dust still, the dry brick kiln-colored, soft still like milkweed pollen swirls of spring caught in eddies, as the whirlpooling wind caught the ground, as the bat caught the sweetspot, cracked the ball, caught the kid unsuspecting, sifting the red dirt with tongue-wet fingers. Catching me surprised and stillborn with my fouled fair hopes for a winning season.

For no knowable reason, it's the national pastime. Resilience and risk. Muscle and mayhem. Settle the dust and play ball.

Between Hell
and
High Water

Gynecology

The speculum leers, moistens
Its gaping lips. Readied antiseptically
For the cold kiss, loveless.
My bridal bed of unfurled paper sheeting
Freshly ready for the science of virgin blood
And telltale cells scraped on slides
Frozen and sent to labs, seen
By eyes that never knew me.
Samplings of inside, born in cold light
Dyed visible under fluorescence,
Lurid green, red embarrassments.
Your gloved hand parts the curtain,
The flimsy gown, enters
Followed by the rest of you.
Schooled to probe and diagnose blind
Touch this and that part
Hidden in fold on fold.
I presuppose rogue growth, suspicious anomaly
Feeding and replicating, awaiting
Uncovering, numb discovery.
My eyes meander upward, tallying
Indentations of soundproofed ceiling tiles
Sensing the traveling circuit where latex fingers
Discern dimensions, tissues unexceptional,
And after all, anatomically correct.
Interior repose, functions stop and start
With lunar logic, the lizard brain

Behaving, autonomous.
Your medicine now knows me biblically.
And what generations of undifferentiated bodies
Will follow me to this marriage bed,
What progeny will issue from this encounter
Joining sapiential plunge
And passive flesh.
You stand beside my prone human half
Haloed in halogen light and sharp instruments sterilized,
Your notetaking attendant in tow, expressionless.
So what will we learn today, doctor
With the suave lean hands and the limpid bedside manner?
What prognosis this morning, of the weak weaker
Sex?
I fear it.
I dread it.
And I can't wait.

Confessions of a Gutter Snipe

The mist carries gull droppings
carries the stampede of nasal scree.
Typical Pacific. The land lies slouching
back bumps on Cascade's callous.
The three longest toes rubbing the seventy piers.
The blood blisters, trigger-fingers nicotine stained.
I will lay myself down in a sidestreet
westbound with the oil-fish sun, slicked,
hidden by puddling towers
shadows worried by moody blue afternoon.
Soon
just before the time changes
and it's earlier. Or later than before,
than ever,
just before cloud-break and rainbow-bend,
I'll plunge, Seattle-style. And the settling in
a whole half
hour dreamfree,
when you'll lay me down, your ear
scanning my skin for pulse
with your footpressed thumbscrew
ground in grounds.
I pant with the wait
on the curb, panhandling clear sky and loose change.
I play to slay or be slain, until
the coffee breaks, my eyes
inverse mirrors of thirst
unscratchable itch.

We are both conspirators in this,
exiled, wandering wills careening with sundown
upwind's whim.

I give you up for lost beyond my blind knife's blunt edge
at last lost in San Juan's island swill
lost rim-shelf's hills sinking
lost whales warbling offshore
intent on the long-lost longboat passage north by northwest
savagely surrender-stained, hard-pressed
the uncountable cost, trashcans smoldering
the fading fire
the lost last chance for dilapidated bliss
the lost empire of constant rain.

Terrorism of the Heart:
Confessions of an Al Qaeda Operative

No matter what
I will slide between the skids
Of your sleepy security,
The innocent adolescent geography of dream cornfield angst,
Try as you will to screen me
With trellises of light
And the brass buckles of starched musclemen.
No real impediment to my cave-painted training,
Guerilla tactics to seduce your rest,
Smelling your skin unnoticed, so closely do I pass.
My weapon won't expose any x-ray yet invented
Never signal clangs of alarm
Through your cautiously roped corridors of arterial tissue.
And I'll advance smoothly
Soundlessly invisible in the crowd
Of accidental tourists and hamstrung virgins,
Scimitar huddled in my curious curl
Of smirk and faint praise.

No matter what
I will slide between the sheets of fugitive faces most wanted
Like sheets of cheap cotton behind dead-bolted bedrooms.
And teased by my touch so light
So nuclear
You'll never notice I entered not once,
But twice,
And never recover.

No matter the risk, the price
I'll blend with the blind skittering passengers,
Set sail off the soft-landing tarmac,
Letting go of ground and guts and God.

No matter what, I'll slap this jet
Through your proud twin towers' pout
And in a bonfire of jihad-mad ash
I will sear your heart well done
For the carnivorous and heaven-hungry Allah.
And once before remorse's last spite
I will please my mouth and savor one bite.

Dairy Diary

I will milk my obsession like a cow's teat.
Roll and squeeze.
Roll and squeeze.
Please tell me now
is she the one with the tortoise shell clip corraling
her hair, riverweed layered
in leftovers of Pampas grassland generations, or spiced
with the sauerkraut of Dresden butchers,
strings of cabbage and pickled,
the aroma of rye.
Or perhaps the slim shy androgene with knubby
Peruvian pancho, llamas cavorting in acrylic,
rhythmic Inca indications.

Perhaps not. Her feet,
though clean, are dark
and reminiscent of Andean dust, and I know
you like your cafe
con leche
especially in the morning.

Puberty

To be naked at Starbuck's, slimmed to skin,
Is not so wrong, is it?
The need to be nude nowhere
More urgent than beneath
The coffee clouds and lemony
Chiffon meringue music's sweet parsing,
Nibbling bites of latte skimmed
To our ears.
No. No
Other joy rides through Coventry lanes bareback
Humming flesh straddling horsehide,
Lady Godiva sunstruck in blonde.

Did your mother notice
My shy needs, nude niceties
Costuming rare scraped seeds
Glistening, or the clumsy mime
Dressing, redressing the welts in real time.
The wounds I bear
I bare for you
Only.

I think she knew.

Emilia Not

I am not Emilia
And I can't remember if her hair
Is a Mediterranean mix of russet and pine and curl and straight
Or Indian black and pampas wheat.
How endless were the nights when she'd wait
For your call, to clutch the phone minutes after blue midnight
With your voice rippling down the caverns of pink inner ear
Waiting all day to hear her name inflected off your tongue singing
The phone ringing rousing those sleeping down the hall, or spoonlike
    beside her.
But deaf to caution she'd catch the place and time
Before night's silence resumed its cushioned gait
And the sleeping limbs settled again as she passed the hours rehearsing
    breakfast.

No, I am not Emilia
And I can't retrieve your whisper's sonorous lilt
Or moonglint of eye or shock of sunheated skin
Or hinted promises of more to come some unclaimed day.
Can't recall what suppers shared or picnic lunch
Complete with loaf of bread and jug of wine
Red and dry and honeysweet thou.

No, I am not
Emilia's skin carbon-stained with your fingerprints
Emilia's thighs remembering your weight, circumferential girth
Emilia's dreams singing "A kiss is a tango for two mouths
An Argentinian tangle of tongues and lips..."
Emilia's greedy guilt, her uphill heaving approach
Her downsliding surrender.

No, I am not Emilia.
Fewer syllables spike my name
Creeping time crepes my skin
Lighter eyes tallying less, dreaming more.
I can never offer Emilia's freedom of speech, freedom
Of pressing limbs, the perfect freedom
Of Emilia preaching abandonment.
Abandoning us both, oozing consciousness brings blemishes to light
Hyperdermically.
And you foreswear the cozy concupiscence of forbidden fruit
Abandoning the familiar meal of skin that tastes of pomegranates.

No, I am not Emilia.
But now, even Emilia
Is Emilia no longer.

Between Sleep
and
Walking

Amber Bed

I am trapped in a glaze of licorice chewed blond,
A slice of rock, sweet honey.
Sap secretions oozed eons ago
When elms and birch trumpeted hegemony,
Skyscraping canopy
Fierce forest floor.
Caught in mid-oracle,
A denuded insect,
Wings tweaked by mean boys,
Or a genetic aberration of frazzled fern
Unsymmetrical, obscure and extinct
Ground beneath a heedless heel.
Once upon some sunshine, profuse and extravagant,
Sugar maple's leachings staining bark,
Syrup's tang for no one's tongue.
Dazzling only in fossilized format,
Relic of unheard miracle
Falling on deaf ears.
But I am still your bitter honey,
And you are still my sullen rock,
Meager miser withholding jewels,
Naked neck still nesting
Anticipating the falling blade,
The indifferent avalanche of amber.

Bed of Twisting and Turning

The reign of late summer hangs ferocious
from flung petals parted by sap and seethe –
Everyone forgets the risk of wetted

roads, the predictable snake of puddling.

If I could live the drops by longitude, tracking
the earth's curl north with the four lanes, maybe
I could trail your road past the sweet

corn, the filament silk, the green fingers

pointing crookedly, limning your curvaceous iteration.

Maidenbed

I was taught shame at five at my mother's knee,
only as high as the hem of her shift, her decorous hand,
a hand's length up from the last curve of calf

muscle. The taut shame of underwear uncovered under sky,
the nasty underneath my crinoline, my fullcut poodle skirt.
No real dog with bark and slobber, just gumball pink

tongue and tail, and grey-felt flanks that felt
jelly-smooth and jolly, covering all that muss
and smell of flushed toilets

and little girl grime.

Just a day when shame sneaks in hungry and young once
in the wake of flirts on the brink, comparing cup sizes
and cramps. Rapt with the smell of estrogen in the morning,

no brag of mine could match this, only flounce
of skirt, eerie like a sine curve, could bring
my ersatz punctuation – an encoded reply: rabbit briefs

bouncing eyelet on the breeze.

More than a hologram, she shimmered
approaching, chill before rain. My skirt's cur's yap
now chastened, heeled and yanked back

toward sobered self. "Ladies, ladies,
ladies never show their underwear." Underneath
all that undercover mischief sent packing

exiled underground between the folds of musk
and latent menses, shame's vapor rising from the taut pull
the tight lacing, strictures enforced, sent

to bed without supper.

These days of thongs when lace flows over
the boudoir's brim, threads entangled in the olive wood,
my truant face within the mirror's glass earned,

leering shame learned.

Silent Bed

She is leaving and leaving
me cold. Nothing, nothing
doing. She and her lyre and the liar

she is. Cipher, placeholder for speaking
throats, eulogy for extinction.
The words remember

where a being breathed. She

erects epics
by committee, mimes rhapsodes strumming
strings of Ionian gut, skims

the shallow riptides of Lesbos for shells. Eponymous
like other shirked wives, left
holding the loom while their crabbed

husbands slum with sorcerers.

Tongueless in the thunderous
hereafter. Awkward orchid
moments, flaming yet harder

to swallow than chortling pits. Bitter
anise and lavender, fragrant
with the purple passages

in Proust's thudding prose.

Sun Bed

Just a few days behind the solstice trap
door, sun sighs and traipses south
again. We slouch with the heat, pores evaporating,

sun won't set soon enough.

Dusk transmogrified and sinuously long, why
won't dark ever dawn and take the glare away
beneath its hardened shell? The sheets

hiss in the heat. Even naked we can't
comfort find or a cool enough place skin
has yet to cook. If you touch me

I will sizzle.

Death Bed

Today I brought home her make-up, half
used lipsticks, gummed mascara, a blush
brush with clots of color still clinging, skin

fragrance, particles of living face still

clinging. In my sleep I heard the soft shirring
and turned and thrashed for hours until
I had to toss every listless item, every

bristle out. Otherwise, I'd make relics, rebuild

her whole life from start, one DNA molecule at a time.

Sleighbed

Snowbound sleighbed horsebells droving the leapyear's ice, fattens the pond – white chocolate chilled pudding skin. So frigid the voile sheets, the bedsprings creak, pipes crack. We sneak toward the summer house in winter.

Solstice shrinks the inching hours. Rolling north through Anatolia – checkmate for outlaws, the perfect escape for creatures driven by too much sun and south and olivepress viscosity. Turbid and heat-tossed, insouciant insomnia.

Only the iceglass sheen, breath on the windowpane stained with letters once described, erased with a woolballed fist. Self-effacement precedes laurel-lading. The fading flesh, eluding mind, dim heat.

I'd rather twist stitches from this quilt – my mother's hands' winter's work -- and sniff snow coming: a fox, silver-tipped around the curtained corner.

Harem Bed

I am sick of the veiled life and your backfiring intentions. I signal you my hero with the others. New women and women made grey in the service of groomed scimitars traveling between the curtain's swirl and the world's brisk breath. I am hidden like pending trauma. A private part pathologically deprived and cinched, cordoned off from the rip and tide, late summer Sahara.

Yes, still part of you, My Lord, and your dozing convent, lazing in the catnip, the granules of balsam. Syllables of resistance, prayers and spat slander, sewn like unripe berries in the folds of my veil.

Still in bed at noon. Tousled silk and stretchpants, broadcasting my flamboyant modesty, my chaste musk.

Soundproof Bed

The soundproof bed. Haunt of poverty, oak cask of plenty. Curled
between the armored flanks, the damasked sheets. Your perfume reminds
me of tidewater, ticklish and curious. Beach sand in my bed, arabesques
of tar like spread jam.

The sun beats along the centuries' throb. How now the Aegean after these
greedy eons? I shot arrows like spiders into the waves, each embroidered
with a valentine for the You of the epochal moment, magnetic flux. Some
floated with crumbs and condoms, pale parade of inner-city night-love
jazzed flotsam and jetsam. Daisy petals of a harder thunder – He loved
me, loved me not.

Knotted like laurel crowns, sprint victory floating out with the spring
tide. Bodies, spent needles, needless lovenotes in beer bottles. Find me,
night blooming jasmine dream of a night, as close as my neighbor's
aralias, as distant as your alternate universe. A parallel, micro-
mirrorworld of makeup and mascara, made-up dreamdates, making up
after the afternoon rain.

Tomorrow is laundry day. Sand and snails, surfsounds and tidal
organisms, odalisque dreams down the drain.

See-through Bed

I don't care that the moon wanes without me
watching, grazing its third quarter over my shoulder
like a miffed sniff and tug of toga

trailing west with its cratered horn
of plenty. I can't keep caring
how days trip over the heels

of tiresome nights, Tuesday's irksome commute
eclipsing Friday's flirty wink, delirious
with deliverance denied. Not much

consolation in the smacking lips
of this spring morning, appetite churning
destined to die hungry, fruit of the vine

left to rot or never ripen; full maturity, some
trite illusion. Pale
chimera of the lunatic morning.

My neighbor flies the flag
of watermelon, sliced
in wedges, seeds showing. It must be

summer in their house already, charcoals
on the grill, roasting meats
in the air

at twilight, late.

Bed of Surrender

I am the mangled wing hunk and haunch of joint
no loose sloughed feather flurried or delicate frond
lifting with morning but a chewed animal wedge
torn from spiraling torso sinking with gravity.
No more yesterday's aerial circuitry or morning yoga,
awaking to toned muscle movement, surveying dawn
clouds still dreaming. Snake. Cathedral. Smoking
club conversation and French wine. Ground
is what comes when the predator becomes prey.
Startling slap of decent life collapsed, sponge
on earth absorbing the last of the rain. Patterns
of fringe soaked spread like a Japanese fan
silk tracings and embroidery, the prayer
of moistened geisha hands.

Miles distant where you spend unreconciled nights,
rising days unfolding, dwindling, does a one-winged
creature earth-exiled, picking some precarious way
through blown scraps and crumbs cross your path? Distracted
dilated pupils pilfering details, surfing sky blind
to the crutching at ground level not far
from your footsteps.

Pain mostly gone, only occasional tremors where
the wing was and only when I gaze sideways
and notice the absence. So I will learn to fly
skewed, and try not to look.

Bed of Nails

Tonight you gave me back the moon, approaching
its fullness, hued pumpkin as if to warm
the chill and croon. It won't be long till

fall comes, sifting leaves and harvest.

You give me back my lines, my lives
tonight – to be the one you'd invite
to the stage door and casting calls

early. We speak as friends, patois of cellular affinity.

With you here I retrieve myself, as you ready
to go, with the buffalo's dust north toward
autumn and the oven-hidden loaves.

Corn ripens as we speak, we sleep;
home is only one wheatfield

away.

Photo Art: MJ Maxwell

C.M. Clark's poetry has appeared in a variety of publications, including *Gulf Stream* magazine, the Florida Center for the Literary Arts anthology *Write Here*, and she is a frequent contributor to the online journal, *Asili*. She has also been involved in a number of multimedia collaborations with other artists, including "COMPLEMENT/Art Basel," a video project, as well as "Now Taste This," an event pairing poets and gourmet chefs. Her work has been published in the recent collection *Pillow Talk*, a joint project with painter Georges LeBar, and she has appeared at the Miami Book Fair International as part of the Write Out Loud Cafe. Clark lives in Miami, Florida with her husband and daughters.

www.ingramcontent.com/pod-product-compliance
Lightning Source LLC
LaVergne TN
LVHW011411080426
835511LV00005B/477